MW01156985

Ray,

So... thinking about these books what the Guv wrote, I wondered if we might get in on the act a bit. I've knocked this up by remembering things the Guv's said about stuff and thought we could maybe send it to his publishers, get a cut of the proceeds. What do you think? Have a look through, see if there's anything I've missed and then we can tidy it up a bit.

Chris

I think you'll be wearing your knacker-sack as a cap when the Guv sees it. Worth a try though I suppose.

Ray

The
WIT and WISDOM
of
DCI GENE HUNT

BANTAM PRESS

LONDON · NEW YORK · TORONTO · SYDNEY · AUCKLAND

Police Records Archive
Entry# F7W-TH-Y11W-BRK/RD

TRANSWORLD PUBLISHERS
61–63 Uxbridge Road, London W5 5SA
A Random House Group Company
www.rbooks.co.uk

**First published in Great Britain in 2009 by Bantam Press
an imprint of Transworld Publishers**

ISBN 9780593065075
2 4 6 8 10 9 7 5 3 1

Copyright © Kudos Film and Television
Limited 2009

Kudos Film and Television Limited has
asserted its right under the Copyright, Designs
and Patents Act 1988 to be identified as the
author of this work.

This book is a work of fiction and, except in
the case of historical fact, any resemblance
to actual persons, living or dead, is purely
coincidental.

Life on Mars is a Kudos Film and Television
Limited production for BBC Wales. Executive
Producers: Claire Parker, Jane Featherstone and
Matthew Graham.

Ashes to Ashes is a Kudos Film and Television
Limited production in association with
Monastic Productions for BBC Wales.
Executive Producers: Simon Crawford Collins,
Jane Featherstone, Matthew Graham, Ashley
Pharoah and Alison Jackson.

Life on Mars © Kudos Film and Television
Limited 2005. Original first series broadcast on
BBC television, January 2006.

Ashes to Ashes © Kudos Film and Television
Limited 2007. Original first series broadcast on
BBC television, February 2008.

BBC and the BBC logo are trademarks of the
British Broadcasting Corporation
and are used under licence.
BBC logo © BBC 1996

Writer: Guy Adams
Designer: Lee Thompson
Editorial Guru: Sarah Emsley
Editorial Angel: Manpreet Grewal

This book is sold subject to the condition that
it shall not, by way of trade or otherwise, be
lent, resold, hired out, or otherwise circulated
without the publisher's prior consent in any
form of binding or cover other than that in
which it is published and without a similar
condition, including this condition, being
imposed on the subsequent purchaser.

A CIP catalogue record for this book is
available from the British Library.

Addresses for Random House Group Ltd
companies outside the UK can be found at:
www.randomhouse.co.uk
The Random House Group Ltd
Reg. No. 954009

The Random House Group Ltd makes every
effort to ensure that the papers used in its books
are made from trees that have been legally
sourced from well-managed and credibly
certified forests. Our paper procurement policy
can be found at: www.randomhouse.co.uk/
paper.htm

Typeset in BigBlox & Baskerville.

Printed and bound in Italy.

www.kudosfilmandtv.com
www.bbc.co.uk/lifeonmars
www.bbc.co.uk/ashestoashes

CONTENTS

The WIT and WISDOM of DCI GENE HUNT

DC CHRIS SKELTON
(and DS Ray Carling)

how crap is that? Needs something more clever. How about than a hooker has scabs? —

Jesus! You sound like you're four or something! DIS IS A BUK ABUT STUFF WOT IS GUD. —

What happens after beer and before women? Half an hour trying to get the little constable to stand to attention?! Should put that in, be bloody funny that. Missed opportunity.

INTRODUCTION
DC CHRIS SKELTON

(and DS Ray Carling)

DCI Gene Hunt is a man with more opinions than most people have had hot dinners.

He has already written two books explaining how to do policing and that. This time his genius is turned on the world at large.

The Wit and Wisdom of DCI Gene Hunt is a book that provides both education and insight into the mind of a man who is very clever.

the Guv's

Here you will find ~~DCI Gene Hunt~~'s opinions on everything from beer to women and all that is in between.

and without ————
his bloody
knowledge!

Or toilet ("words
go in best while ————
turds fall out"...
Shakespeare said
that, I think, or
maybe Churchill...)

Compiled by the ~~man~~ ^{men} who know him most
(intimately.) Listed alphabetically this is the
ultimate collection of the man's quotes and
opinions.

sounds gay that

The Wit and Wisdom of DCI Gene Hunt
belongs in every man's library.

DC Chris Skelton - Editor

DS Ray Carling - Better Editor

ARRESTING PEOPLE

DCI Hunt wouldn't have got far in this job unless he'd arrested a lot of people.

The process of an arrest is a very precise affair with very specific guidelines.

How come you still have a job then?

Perhaps nobody ever told the Guv that!

I don't get many people resisting arrest. Once they've seen me in all my horrible glory, a prison cell takes on an attractive light. At least they'll be safe there...

I used to think being... a policeman was like being an old Western sheriff, making the streets a safe place. Having spent the last twenty years banging up scum I realize it's more like being a human toilet brush. My old mum would be so proud.

Anything you say will be taken down, ripped up and shoved down your scrawny little throat until you choke to death.

Have I arrested a lot of people?
Put it this way: how many coppers do you know who wear out an average of three sets of handcuffs a year?

Everyone needs a hobby in life. Some peoplo colloct stamps and put them in an album, some collect coins and put them in a case. I collect crooked bastards and put them in the nick.

BIRTHDAYS

Birthdays, we all have them.

You won't have any more if you don't beef up these intros, pal. Have you even read a book?

Birthdays are like blowjobs: a man can never have too many.

I don't get many cards on my birthday. I suppose most people I meet on the job are pissed off I'm still alive.

What do you buy the man who has everything? Something to wash it down with!

Birthdays are a celebration of getting old, and I honour the event by practising for the future: shouting random bollocks, embarrassing everyone in public and losing my bladder control at regular intervals.

The best way to enjoy your birthday is to do the reverse of what you did on your first: climb inside a woman.

Birthdays are like fat birds – nobody likes to admit how many they've had.

Some bloke thought it would be funny to try and give me 'the bumps' at my birthday bash last year, so I gave him some straight back. He didn't look 148 when I started, but he bloody well did by the time I'd finished.

I always forget other people's birthdays. It's just cheaper that way.

I'll never forget how exciting it was to finally hit eighteen... now, by law, nobody could stop me doing what I'd been doing for years.

BOOKS

DCI Gene Hunt has written two books already, so it's not surprising he has something to say on the subject of ~~literoo literyat letrech~~ books.

Yeah... like how much will you pay me to write a third?

I always find it strange that I've ended up writing books, I didn't think I had it in me. I went out with an English teacher once but she was always disgusted by my improper use of the colon.

Books are great at opening the mind, especially the phone directory – if you get a good swing going you can really do some damage.

They say some people always have their nose in a book. I knew someone like that once, a drug dealer, one of his customers had cut it off and shoved it in there.

Books are great, they make the lav look nice and offer a lot more absorbency than you'd think.

They say the pen is mightier than the sword. I'm not convinced myself, although a pen can be a very effective tool in an interrogation.

Libraries are brilliant: they cost nothing, you take whatever you fancy then bring it back when you're bored. If only they did them for wives.

I haven't read many books. To be honest, there's always something more interesting to do – breathing, sleeping, scratching my arse...

People love detective books, don't they? Not that I read them myself – that would be like handing a copy of **Egg Sucking: An Advanced Guide** to my grandma.

The problem with murder mysteries is that they give the public an idea that they're clever enough to do police work. In reality, they could no more solve a murder than knit with their own arsehole...

I'll slip
this one
in too!
R.

Chris — We need some pictures — all these words are doin' my head in. Especially some of Drake showin' some leg...

I've got these ones of the Guv in a pub, and having a drink — they alright?

BOOZE

Like all of us, DCI Gene Hunt likes a little drink now and then.

Little? Speak for your-bloody-self.

You got the D.T.s? Pour yourself a large Scotch, that should sort you.

Beer is one of the vital food groups – the others, of course, being fags, fanny and a few forkfuls of curry.

Some people drink to forget. I can't remember why I do it.

Some people say I drink too much. Not sure I understand their point, it seems like saying someone breathes excessively.

If God hadn't wanted men to wake up in the gutter some days he wouldn't have stuck tits on barmaids.

Drinking decent Scotch is an evolutionary process, there to weed out the weak, the tasteless and the tight.

I knew a bloke once who lost both hands in a threshing machine, the poor bastard. He got over it, never could hold his drink, though.

When it comes to women you've got to love gin, it saves all that need for charm...

I used to look down on wine but that was just because I hadn't drunk enough of it. It's hard to look down on something when you're lying on the floor.

Apparently drink makes you depressed.
Maybe I'm doing it wrong, but it always
cheers me up no end.

Drinking mates are the best friends you can
have. They're a laugh while you're in the pub
but have the decency to forget your drunken
antics by the morning.

I always drink in moderation. I'm not an idiot, once I'm unconscious it's time to stop.

I realised I had a serious drink problem the
other day when the off-licence was closed.
How much more serious does it get?

When I was married, the wife always used to
complain about my drinking. She didn't mind
me popping out for the odd pint, but why did
I have to be rolling drunk every night? I tried
to explain... there's nothing worse than a job
half done.

Apparently drinking knackers your liver...
Well, what can I say? It knackers your wallet
too, but life is full of sacrifices.

Don't you just hate people who say, 'I don't
drink to get drunk.' That's like saying, 'I
don't get in my car to drive anywhere.'

People have funny expressions for getting
drunk, especially 'getting arseholed'. This
is not something I'd ever have an ambition
for, to be honest – I'd like to think there's not
enough booze in the world for that to end up
on my agenda.

Why is it that middle-aged housewives
always moan when their husbands go out and
get drunk of an evening? Don't they realize
they'd never get any sex if they didn't?

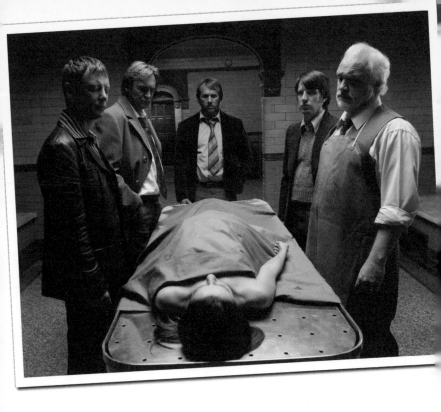

did you cut me out of this one, Ray?

it's a photo of a proper
copper, you don't quite make it

us lot, in a morgue, with a stiffy.

It's a STIFF, you div!

BREAKING THE BAD NEWS

Sometimes in this job you have to be the bearer of sad news.

Not everyone puts it as nicely as the Guv.

Like, 'Sorry, Mrs Skelton, but your son's a div'

Hiya love, DCI Hunt, how are you feeling? I've just come to talk to you about how your brother copped it.

If there's a hell, he's going there and will be poked up the arse with sharp, fiery sticks, for ever and ever, amen.

I know it must be hard for you to hear your husband died in such circumstances. Still, think of it this way – as a dirty bloody pervert, wrapped in cling-film and choking on a donkey was just the way he would have wanted to go.

It's not all bad. Is your son's room big enough to take a lodger?

What's that? He was an Organ Donor? I don't think that's going to make any difference – even Bernard Matthews wouldn't know what to do with what's left of your husband.

There's no easy way to tell you this, so I just brought some pictures. Your husband's the blackened, crispy one.

Did you know your husband was into blokes? About six inches, according to the coroner.

Death comes to us all in the end, love, though I hope when my time comes I'm not screaming like a baby while my knackers are being fed into a meat slicer. Your son certainly got the thin end of the wedge there...

Good news and bad news – the good news is your son's not dead. Bad news is your cooking's going to be a bit limited from now on, unless you can think of something other than soup that you can eat through a straw?

Bad news is like a dose of crabs – giving it to someone else always ends in tears.

I'm afraid we're going to need you to identify her body. I know it seems a terrible idea, but it can be a very important part of the grieving process and a valuable chance to say a final goodbye. Before we waste the petrol though, are you one hundred per cent sure you'd know her left foot if you saw it again?

Try not to dwell on the how or why of it, that's our job... though we're offering five to one on 'knife up the jacksy from an angry hooker' if you want a cut of the action?

Look, love, I know you must be gutted but think positively. A beautiful woman like you... you can choose to look at this as a tragedy or a fresh start. What are you up to next Thursday?

I would like to stress that we don't know for sure that your wife was having an affair, sir. I mean, she was giving the bloke a blow-job when the car crashed but – who knows? – maybe she was just thinking of you and saving a cab fare.

I'm sure he was thinking of you at the end. Probably not right at the end, mind... If I had to guess I'd say his final thought was more along the lines of 'that bastard's not really going to hit me in the face with that axe is he?'

CARS

All blokes love their motors, our cars are as much a part of us as our legs. Just quicker getting us places!

Was that a joke? Jesus! We'd have more laughs if Colonel Gaddafi wrote the introductions.

Fire up the Quattro!

Take that seat-belt off! You're a police officer, not a bloody vicar.

My ex-wife complained that I loved my car more than her, which just goes to show she wasn't as stupid as you might think. There's never any doubt which one I most wanted to get inside of, that's for sure.

Two skinheads made a right mess of my bonnet the other day. Maybe next time I should try and swerve.

They say a man's car is an extension of his dick, which is all very well until you try and park.

Cars are a bit like women. We've all had to put up with some old bangers in our time because the beautiful ones cost a lot of money to run.

It's stunning to look at, handles well and takes your breath away when you're riding it. My car's not bad either.

I've always been a natural behind the wheel of a car, I think it's because I'm not a bloody woman.

CHRISTMAS

Ho Ho Ho!

Tit Tit Tit...

I don't think I ever believed in Father Christmas. In Manchester a fat, hairy man sneaking into your house at night isn't something to look forward to.

We didn't celebrate Christmas in our house. Goodwill to all men was not something I liked to encourage in the ex-Mrs Hunt – she got like that after too many Bacardis anyway.

The only way I can imagine a fir tree ending up in our front room is if we had a hurricane and the bastard came in through the window.

My parents always told me Father Christmas would only come if I was a good boy. It never really seemed worth changing my lifestyle for a pair of socks and a tangerine.

Christmas is where unpopular food goes to die... sprouts, dates, satsumas, that chewy fruit snot in icing sugar...

I've a lot of sympathy for Father Christmas. Having been married I know what it's like to only come once a year.

It's the season to be jolly apparently. Burglaries go up, domestics go up, the number of mad drunks laying into one another on the streets goes through the roof – maybe it's just me, but I struggle in the hunt for chuckles.

What's the spirit of Christmas? Brandy, I suppose. It sure as hell isn't Advocaat, that's just alcoholic snot in a glass.

I went home bladdered last Christmas Eve and the missus insisted I stuff the turkey. It was the best offer I'd had in years, and sure as hell better than the alternative.

They feed you sprouts at Christmas and then complain about the inevitable smell – hardly fair, is it? It's like getting a blind man to juggle a dinner service and then whining about breakages.

I had this fat, roasted bird last Christmas. Looked a bit suspect but was blinding once you tucked into it. Sonya, I think her name was.

My ex-wife kept going on about me buying her a watch for Christmas. I told the greedy cow, 'There's a clock on the cooker and one on the bedside table, what d'you need another for?'

Christmas is a great time for party games. There are all the favourites: Pin the Tail on the Donkey, Blindman's Buff, Oh Shit, I've Finally Snapped and Struck the Mother-in-Law with a Carving Knife, What Shall I Do With the Dead Bitch Now?

Christmas rots your guts and empties your wallet. It should be declared a disease, not a public holiday.

I've no problem with the idea of shoving treats in stockings, just as long as the woman in question's still wearing them.

CRIMINALS

If there's one thing Gene Hunt knows a lot about it's criminals.

Thanks for that, D.C. Bleeding obvious, you'll be telling us Frankie Howerd knows a lot about toilet cubicles next.

He's an unpleasant little scrotum, what we in the business call a necessary evil.

Murderers do not play tennis!

Softly, softly catchee bent bastard.

They say that a lot of criminals are just disadvantaged people. Once I've finished with 'em they're generally right!

A lot of criminals have a bad history. Their future ain't looking too rosy either.

There's a lot of talk about looking into the mind of a criminal and I'm all for it. Give me a baseball bat and a hacksaw and I'll gladly take a peek.

Criminals must be stupid, how else do you explain their career choice when they know I'm in town?

I've got a lot of sympathy for criminals. After all, I know exactly what's going to happen once I've laid my hands on them.

I feel the same about criminals as a plumber feels about turds.

DRUGS

DCI Hunt hasn't much sympathy for those caught up in drugs.

That's like saying Hugh Hefner doesn't mind looking at tits.

Drugs make you forgetful, make you talk funny, make you see things that aren't there. My old grandma got all of that for free when she had a stroke.

Smackheads, when I come calling you'll discover the clue is in the name.

I've got the perfect hit for junkies, I make it from my right fist.

'Chasing the dragon'? That's a laugh, most of 'em couldn't chase their own farts.

If it's weird visions you're after, may I suggest Camden at kicking-out time? It doesn't get weirder than that.

A lot of junkies take drugs to escape the real world. They should just get a coach to Bournemouth, it's a damn sight cheaper.

People take cocaine to give them confidence. I must be easily pleased – splash of Brut and I'm damn near unstoppable.

Apparently pot makes you relaxed. I don't see it myself, all the potheads I meet are in a right agitated state. Mind you, at the time I'm often chasing them around their front rooms setting fire to their hair. Maybe that puts them off the relaxing they were doing before I turned up.

EDUCATION

**You don't get to be a man like Gene Hunt
without years of learning.**

*Whereas you were born thick and just
keep getting worse*

It doesn't take a degree in applied bollocks to
know what's going on.

I learnt a lot of skills at
school that set me up for life
– smoking, drinking and how
to unclip a woman's bra one-
handed. I think our education
system's the best in the world.

I was always in trouble at school, but then
when you're surrounded by the cast of **St
Trinian's** it's going to happen, isn't it?

When I was caught selling porn mags as a kid the headmaster promised me six of the best. He wasn't lying either – that was some specialist stuff, I cut him in for twenty per cent (only fair).

A lot of people had a teacher that really inspired them at school. For me, it was Madame Bovert. She taught French, and swallowed.

Some people reckon you never stop learning. In my experience most people never start.

FIGHTING

In our line of work you often have to be handy with your fists. There are plenty of people on the streets who are only too happy to take a pop at a police officer and you have to be ready to fight back. *Or just better armed.*

Black suits you, do you want an eye in the same colour?

I've always been able to handle myself. I'm good in a fight, too.

Talking about fighting fair is as stupid as talking about American intelligence. The key to a fistfight is simple: break them before they've had a chance to blink.

I learnt all I needed to know about fighting from my father. A strong right hook is good, but being handy with a broom handle's even better.

Apparently some people are lovers, not fighters. Why restrict yourself?

When fighting a man, it's important to know his weak points. My wife always aimed for the wallet, but then she never did play fair.

Growing up in Manchester, you had to learn how to fight. It's what the blokes did at the end of every night out. It was that or dancing, and we knew where our strengths lay.

Come last in sex but first in a fight – the true man's creed.

I've never walked away from a fight. I've run away from a few though.

the Guv, with bacon butties on his mind

Drake's tastier!

Ray had a really old curry in the back of his car

it was from the night before and you didn't complain when you were eatin' it!

FOOD

We all need food and sometimes DCI Hunt says things about it.

This is getting worse! Are you worried you'll pass out if you're too funny?

This is Trafford Park. You've as much chance of finding herbs as an ostrich with a plum up its arse.

I tried cooking once. I won't say much about the experience but will pass on some advice: never deep-fry baked beans, they won't thank you for it.

If only someone would invent the edible fag filter, think of the time and ashtrays we'd save.

You've got fingers in more pies than a leper on a cookery course.

They say the way to a man's heart is via his stomach. It's out by a few inches, to be honest, but if the woman gets that far I'll happily direct her the rest of the way.

They say you never forget your mother's cooking. This is very true in my case – I'm sure I still have the toxicology reports somewhere.

I don't get these vegetarians. If God hadn't wanted us to eat animals, he wouldn't have made the bastards out of meat.

My wife used to achieve miracles in the kitchen, the most impressive being that nobody died from her damn food.

With a lifestyle like mine, you begin to forget that not all food comes in a foil dish.

The French say the English are obsessed with their meat and two veg. That's a bit rich coming from those randy sods, isn't it?

British food gets a lot of stick for being bland. Well, maybe it is, but that's because we've got better things to get excited about.

If they banned lard, half of Britain would seize up. It's the quality man's lubricant.

The French steam fish, the Spanish dry it, the Germans cover it in salt, and the British? We frigging **batter** it. It's an attitude like that that wins wars.

I tried salad once. Do you know, I don't think I've ever known rage quite like it. I threatened to stab the waiter in the eye with a breadstick unless he brought me a fried animal immediately.

I like to be healthy and not eat too much, just enough to keep the booze down.

FOREIGNERS

The Guv has never pretended to work for the United Nations.

No kidding, Prince Philip makes a better diplomat.

I once hit a bloke for speaking French.

There's nothing wrong with foreigners, it's all just a tragic accident of geography.

Americans hear a lot of jokes about their stupidity, which is unfair. They're far too thick to understand them.

I try not to be unpleasant about Americans but, damn it, it's just so much fun.

Say what you like about importing goods from abroad but we'd be lost without them. We can't make good porn to save our lives.

I eat curry, drink wine and drive an Audi, so what's the fuss? I am truly a man of the world.

Germans get very upset when you mention the war. I don't know what the problem is; at least they didn't come third like the French.

Apparently the French are the best chefs in the world. Yeah right, they'll be saying the Germans are the greatest comedians next.

America, land of the free. Free lunch, if the size of them is anything to go by.

I've never been abroad but my guts are well-travelled – India, China, Italy, Greece – I've shat 'em all.

this is a photo of a PROPER set of coppers, Ray
   don't cut me out, you pillock!

the Guv always has a gun,
cos he's hard as nails.
that poofter Tyler doesn't have
one though. Says it all really.

GUNS

As we all know, there are times when a policeman must be prepared to defend himself ~~against potentially life-threatening assailants.~~

Who shoved a dictionary up your arse?
If you mean 'sods wi' guns' then say it.

Drop your weapons, you're surrounded by armed bastards!

Turning up to a hostile situation without shooters is like standing in a gay bar in your Y-fronts. Sooner or later you're bound to get royally buggered.

It's not that I like running around firing a big bloody gun like I'm John Wayne, it's just... oh no, wait, that's exactly what it is.

Shooting at me is like trying
to trim your own pubes
with your teeth – mad,
unforgivable and bound to end
badly.

Smart-arse psychologists say men treat guns
as a penis substitute. There might be some
truth in this, I suppose – both can get you
into trouble and people certainly scream
when you get them out in public.

If God hadn't wanted men to get carried
away once they have a gun in their hand, he
wouldn't have created Charles Bronson.

One of the most important things in a gun
fight is your aim: you should be aiming to hit
the other bastard before he hits you.

Some liberal sorts think arming police officers is a bad idea that can cause more harm than good. A lot of policemen think shooting these liberal sorts might be the best way of settling the argument.

You can't fault British firearms training – they even tell you which end to hold on to.

They say accidents can happen with guns. We're men for God's sake, we're perfectly used to gripping things that might go off unexpectedly.

Do I ever regret having shot someone? Not as much as I would regret them having shot me...

Blokes have always had great aim, they learn it as a child chasing fag-ends in the urinals.

Apparently, you should never discharge your weapon in anger, which rather limits things. I've never shot someone because they were cheering me up, after all.

KIDS

Who doesn't ~~like~~ ^{hate} kids?

I'm assuming that's what you meant?

Kids: the hangover at the end of the big bottle of Scotch that is sex.

Having kids is important and important things need practice. I'm still at that stage. It seems to me it's all downhill after the initial investment so I'm in no rush.

Whenever you moan about kids, people – usually doe-eyed tarts – make a big fuss about 'you used to be one', which is missing the point. I'm a bloke, love, I still am one so why the hell would I want to start sharing my toys?

I often think about having kids, but my mind pulls out at the last minute. It's the Catholic method.

If I wanted something in my life that wailed all the time, cost a fortune and pretty much guaranteed I'd never get laid again, then I'd re-marry. Who needs kids?

Can you imagine what a little Gene Hunt would be like? Christ, there's not a nursery in the country that could handle the little bastard.

When I was a kid I was loud, violent and always demanding attention. I'd like to say I've changed, but I guess it would be a lie.

If I had a son I would tell him everything I know. And if he was anything like me he wouldn't listen to a word.

LIARS

You meet a lot of liars in this job.

No you don't! Ha! Get it?

You're as fake as a tranny's fanny.

You have to be able to tell when people are lying in this job. I don't like to take risks so I usually just give 'em a slap the minute their mouth moves.

I learnt everything I need to know about lying from playing poker.

People always seem to think they can fool me. I suppose it's just hard for people to accept I'm good looking and intelligent.

You know, if you were Pinocchio, you'd have just poked my eye out.

I have a special psychological method to test whether someone's lying – I threaten to pull their guts out of their arse unless they tell me the truth. Never underestimate the psychology of fear.

You'd think people would have more sense than to lie to me, but then you get nowhere in life overestimating people's intelligence. Most people are thicker than Irish cement, and only too happy to prove it to you.

There's a lot of talk about using lie-detecting machines in this job. It's a good idea. We used to have one at our old nick – car battery and jump leads – which worked every time.

London does
have some
nice things
to look at

London has bridges and big buildings.
We even have our own speedboat.

LONDON

The adopted home of Gene Hunt – he's still trying to get used to it!

Up the Manc Lion!

Westminster – more twat per square inch than a January sale in a whorehouse.

Before I came to London I thought only foul-smelling rats and worms travelled underground in tunnels. Good to be proved right.

People around here like to take the piss out of people, just because of where they come from. Gobby southern poofs.

London's full of famous landmarks – Big Ben, Tower Bridge, Gene's Column – I'm thinking of laying on bus trips for that last one.

There's nothing wrong with London that a good, solid airstrike couldn't fix.

In London everyone's unfriendly, just waiting to take a pop at the first bloke who gets in their way. I fit right in.

Londoners love to spell words differently to how they're pronounced – Ruislip, Holborn, Southwark – just so they can correct you if you get it wrong. I usually just tell them to foulk auff.

Finding a parking space in London is like finding a sausage roll at a bar mitzvah.

Samuel Johnson said that 'when you're tired of London you're tired of life' but then this is the bastard who wrote the first dictionary, so I think we can safely say it didn't take much to excite the boring git.

Apparently in London you're never more than four feet from a rat. By my estimations you're never more than three feet from an absolute arsehole, either.

Not only does London have an extensive bus service but it has the underground, too. Which means there are two ways of paying to sit on your arse getting bloody nowhere.

Living in London you can get absolutely anything. Raped, stabbed, mugged, shot...

I hated London when I first arrived but, like a fart in a lift, you get used to it in the end.

MAGGIE

The one woman Gene Hunt talks about without drooling.

Bet she's filthy though, you can just tell.

I once said, 'There'll never be a woman prime minister as long as I have a hole in my arse.' Going on available evidence we still haven't got one, so the comment stands.

Thatcher is the only person in this country that manages to make me look reasonable.

Imagine being married to it. The cold fronts, the violence, the hair – he's a braver man than me.

Never argue with a woman. If you don't believe me, ask an Argentinian.

You can say what you like about Thatcher, she won't listen.

I'm sure inside Thatcher there's a perfectly lovely woman. No doubt she ate the poor bitch.

A lot of people give Thatcher stick. Once they start using clubs I'll consider joining in. No point in taking unnecessary risks.

I've always had a thing for Thatcher – it's a German landmine my dad brought back from the war.

MANCHESTER

Home of the brave!

And wet poofs called Skelton.

People think that if you come from Manchester you're a mad, violent bastard with an attitude problem. They are, of course, quite right.

Everyone should come from Manchester, it sets you up for all the disappointments in life.

Manchester is the living embodiment of a man – it feeds on curry and beer, takes football far too seriously and smacks you in the gob if you don't treat it with a healthy respect.

I loved Manchester like I loved my ex-wife. It was nasty and smelled foul, but if I didn't do it then nobody would.

It's easy to take the piss out of Manchester. No really, it's **very** easy.

In all seriousness I love the North. There are many reasons, but the main one is that it isn't in the bloody South.

In Manchester we believe in shooting straight, talking straight... in fact, the only thing we struggle with is walking straight, but that's the beer for you.

MEDICAL KNOWLEDGE

The Guv never had any medical training but you pick things up in this job.

Like that redhead in the pub last Thursday! She couldn't wait for me to take down her particulars.

[On being told a victim may have died of a heart attack] Then his heart must've exploded out of his arse – there's blood all down his back.

You don't get all that Agatha Christie stuff in real life, weird poisons and murder weapons made out of ice. When we get the call to poke at a body creamed across 500 yards of rail-track, we don't need Quincey to tell us he might have had a disagreement with the 10.30 to Crewe.

I could have been a doctor. My bedside manner has to be seen to be believed.

I got some stick over the state of a suspect the other day. I had to explain that his condition was none of my doing, but that his face had suffered from a breakout of fists.

I know the workings of the human body intimately. It's been my favourite subject for years.

I was at an autopsy the other day. The pathologist cut the cadaver open to show us what the poor sod had eaten for lunch, at which point half the bobbies in the room showed us what they'd had as well.

MINORITIES

We all know you have to be careful what you say these days so you don't upset the paddies and chinks and that.

Ah! So!

I'm learning to be comfortable in the presence of homosexuals. I'm not quite there yet, but I do spend a lot of time watching films of lesbians, you know, just to build up my tolerance.

I've no problem with minorities. As a Manchester City fan living in London I'm one of 'em.

It's getting very difficult to know what you're supposed to call people these days. Half the words we used five years ago see us up to our necks in it. I've finally decided on a safe method by calling everyone I meet a 'bastard'. You know me, I'd hate to hurt anyone's feelings.

I'm a great believer in equal opportunities for minority groups. I'll slap anyone if they're asking for it.

Of course, the main problem with minorities is that there are so bloody many of 'em.

Haha — Ray as James Bond!

Saucer of milk for the kitty kat, eh?!

Even funnier is you as a div in Lycra!

MOVIES

It's obvious the Guv likes movies, he even used to have a poster of Gary Cooper on his wall.

To the left of the bloody dry rot.

When I was young, the cinema in Manchester was where kids did most of their growing up. We smoked cigarettes, drank beer and showed our girlfriends a thing or two. Thing or three, as long as we were sure the management wouldn't notice. The back row saw more action than **The Bridge Over the River Kwai**.

I love foreign language films, Swedish in particular – filthier than a tramp in a septic tank.

You haven't lived until you've seen Brigitte Bardot on the big screen. Large enough that you'd need a head for heights and a taste for potholing.

After watching **High Noon** as a young lad I realized what I wanted to do with the rest of my life. Unfortunately the only cowboys in Manchester were plumbers, so I had to become a copper instead.

Hollywood can be cruel. Asking Sylvester Stallone to act is like asking a dog to sing.

I learnt everything I ever needed to know about sex from the cinema: if you talk a good game you can sneak in for free, things look more impressive with the lights off, and you can put up with a boring first half as long as you get a good climax. Also, if you keep your head down for a bit after it's finished, you can usually sneak back in and do it all again.

All my heroes came from the cinema – Gary Cooper, Marlon Brando, Stacy the usherette. The things she could do with a choc-ice would have given the managing director of Walls a heart attack.

Films can be like women: the trailers promise the world but the main event can be a let-down.

Policing in the movies is so unrealistic, take **Dirty Harry**, for instance. There's no way you'd catch me dead on a bus.

Superman was lucky he stuck to America. Try poncing around London in that suit and he'd have been fishing bits of cape from his arse for weeks.

I watched **Raiders of the Lost Ark** the other day. It was alright, but I couldn't help but think that Indiana Jones was making a bit of a fuss. Nasty natives, vicious animals, poisonous food – that's an average night out in Manchester.

Copper by day

~~Disco Dancer~~ by night
Poofter with make-up

MUSIC

Never let it be said that the Guv's square! He knows all the happening sounds, the groovy ear jockey.

What the bubbling FUCK are you on about?

Me and the wife like Roger Whittaker. Keep it to yourself, we all have our dirty secrets.

When it comes to pop music I'd find Abba hard to beat. Half of them would be easy to spank, but that's something else entirely.

People say you'll always remember where you were when Lennon was shot. I was working, of course, hanging around with a bunch of divs trying to make the world a better place. I suppose it's a tribute of sorts.

Stevie Wonder's getting very popular these days. Nobody saw that coming, least of all him.

I've never got into that Debbie Harry but if she comes to town I'll certainly try.

Apparently music is the food of love. Wish I'd known, I could have saved a packet on prawn cocktails and steak dinners.

According to Elton John 'Saturday night's alright for fighting'. I'll be there if he will.

Cliff Richard's making a comeback. There are worse crimes – though not many – so I'm having to prioritize.

People are surprised at how popular Punk was, but for me you just had to look at the audience. Anyone clever enough to put a safety pin in his face was going to have the musical taste of a retarded hyena.

'Video Killed the Radio Star' but he only just beat me to it.

A lot of people are inspired by pop music, including me. I'm inspired to get a gun and start shooting some bloody musicians.

Music's all about expressing yourself. It works, too. Nothing says 'I'm a wanker' better than listening to Chris De Burgh.

Nightclub: the collective noun for twat.

Orchestral Manoeuvres in the Dark? Awful manoeuvres up their own arse…

Any music that makes a man want to put on make-up should be treated as a virus, with all affected shot.

A lot of music these days is just for dancing, so it's not really for me. You've more chance of seeing Thatcher strip than me dance, and it would be equally horrible to watch.

OLD PEOPLE

We all grow old, but in the Guv's case it will most likely be kicking and screaming.

Using his colostomy bag as a weapon!

They say there's no cure for old age. The first signs I get I'll be calling on my friend Mr Magnum .45 to prove them wrong.

Wobbly on your legs, unable to think and pissing yourself every five minutes. When I do get old I'll have years of heavy drinking to thank for the practice.

I couldn't bear the idea of spending my last years with a stinking bag that's full of shit hanging off me. Luckily I got divorced, so it should be fine.

Why do they let old people drive? When you can no longer move faster than the speed limit it's not a car you should be climbing into, it's a coffin.

Apparently, old age is a second childhood. Maybe it's just me, but I certainly didn't spend my youth farting solids and shouting in post offices.

Old age isn't kind to women. When your nipples start getting caught in your knicker elastic it's time to call it a day.

I was taught to always respect my elders and I did try, but when your granddad goes loopy and gets done for trying to sodomize a shop-window dummy, respect comes hard. Mind you, according to the arresting officer so did Granddad, so fair play for that I suppose...

You can learn a lot from old people. Like when to just shut up and die.

POLITICS

A man as happy to open his mouth as the Guv is always going to have plenty of opinions on politics.

None of them good.

The National Front are too stupid to set someone up. They could stick a shotgun up my arse and pull the trigger but they'd still miss.

Politicians are the only criminals in London I'm not allowed to arrest. It wouldn't be so bad, but they're some of the very worst.

I could never go into politics, I just don't have the right qualities. I'm honest for a start.

Only the Americans could elect Ronald Reagan. Give it a few years and they'll put Kermit the Frog in the White House.

Politicians need amazing mental powers to do their jobs – the maths on those expense accounts can't be easy.

My Chief Super once told me I needed to be more political in the way I did my job. Never let it be said I don't listen to advice but after a week I was knackered. Making up crime reports, getting pissed and finding people to have kinky sex with really takes it out of you...

The Houses of Parliament... it's no coincidence they use a picture of them to advertise hot, thick sauce.

What do politicians do except sit around moaning and expelling hot air all day? I do that after a vicious curry, but it never got me anywhere.

I try to avoid talking about politics. When you spend most of your day punching people during conversations, you don't want to do the same thing socially.

Is there such a thing as a fair politician? I'd say it's about as likely as finding a sexually athletic nun.

I don't know what London would do without politicians. All the hookers and drug dealers would go out of business.

At least politicians have a sense of humour. Just calling yourself the 'Right Honourable' shows you're up for a laugh.

Chief Whip? Kinky bastards don't even bother to hide it, do they?

I don't want to fall back on all the old clichés about MPs being kinky, untrustworthy, money-grabbing, evil tossers who would stab us all in the back for the price of a large brandy... but they give me no choice.

Trusting a politician's about as sensible as trying to breathe underwater.

PRESS

Gene Hunt isn't a big fan of the press.

Bunch of vultures!

The press never met a good story they weren't willing to make up.

I don't hate all journalists. The dead ones are great.

The only thing of worth I've ever found in a newspaper was a battered saveloy.

The press always bang on about freedom of speech, which would be fine if they actually had something of worth to say.

I don't mind looking at tits in the newspaper, it's the tits that wrote it I can't stand the sight of.

I nearly shagged a journo
once. I'm so ashamed, what
can I say? It was the drink
doing the thinking, I'd never
normally go in for bestiality.

Journalists are famous for the amount
they drink, but that's not surprising
though, is it? How else could you get
through the day doing that for a living?

Becoming a journalist must be depressing.
Still, if the local sewage works and
whorehouse aren't hiring, what choice do
you have?

PROSTITUTES

'Ladies of the night' are a common part of urban policing, you can't move for leather skirts and high heels in some parts of London. Not that the Guv would ever pay for sex. Get it for free in this job!

Prostitution is the fast food of sex. Greasy and bad for you but it fills a hole.

The only difference between a high-class hooker and a cheap one is that you have to check their knickers for lobsters rather than crabs.

Sleeping with a hooker can seriously damage your health. A mate of mine didn't so much get the clap as a whole round of applause.

I used to think it was sad that women would use sex to get money, but then I got married and realized it was a way of life.

Prostitution is pretty much the one thing in life where you hope you only get what you pay for. The optional extras can be hell to shift.

I may be the only man in London to have made a hooker blush. Mind you, I had been chasing her up side streets for half an hour and she was nowhere near as athletic as her occupation might suggest.

You can't trust a working girl's hygiene. I've smelt things in fishnets that would make Captain Birdseye puke.

RELIGION

Gene Hunt isn't a religious man.

The only thing he's ever prayed for is a winner in the Grand National.

I'm not a Catholic myself, Mr Warren, but isn't there something about 'thou shalt not suck off rent boys'?

He's more nervous than a very small nun on a penguin shoot.

You're told to respect other people's beliefs, but that's not healthy in my job. After all, most people I meet believe they can get away with murder.

Religion has caused the most violence in history but we shouldn't take that as a reason for banning it. After all, women must have come a close second.

I knew a very religious girl once. Well, I assume she was religious, she spent a lot of time on her knees.

I've never been a believer. When I was a kid our local vicar always stank of baby-oil and cheap whisky, and as representatives went he was enough to put me off for the rest of my life. Nobody should drink cheap whisky.

Apparently God has eyes everywhere. We have a name for that in my job: peeping Tom. Mind you, if God does see everything we do, I like to think I might have taught him a thing or two.

Praying doesn't work: fact. It's the first thing crooks do when they see me kick their door down, and it's never helped them.

God forgives everything, which is a stroke of luck for me.

If Jesus could turn water into wine, I wish he'd pop down to my local. They seem to be doing it the other way around.

Religion is a tricky area for the police. Normally if a copper meets someone taking orders from an invisible man, you start checking his fridge for body parts.

Jesus could walk on water. I can crawl on beer...

I'd love to believe there was a kindly, wise super-being looking down on all of us. I'd also love to believe I'll be throwing one up Olivia Newton-John by this time tomorrow. Life is full of disappointments, so the best thing is just to get on with it.

Apparently, God created me in his own image. Well, he's a handsome-looking fella, I'll give him that.

I could never be a Christian, I just can't follow the Ten Commandments. I can live without the murdering and stealing, but Christ, have you seen my neighbour's wife? There's not a single man in the street that doesn't covet those tits.

I reckon
they're
banging
each other

And the Lord, he said unto them 'What ponce ordered the squid?'

RESTAURANTS

When you work the shifts we do, you don't have much time for a home life. Food is eaten on the run, and any copper worth his salt knows places that will fill his belly at short notice during unfriendly hours.

And not charge a friggin' fortune! I mean, that Greek place, what are they thinking about charging money for some shit wrapped in leaves, eh? They're having a laugh I can tell you.

My body is a temple – it's an altar built from a stack of bacon butties drenched in masala sauce. Worshippers are advised to bring beer.

People seem to think I don't do posh restaurants, but I can Berni Inn with the best of 'em.

Curry: food of kings and the only form of internal cleansing that doesn't involve hosepipes and grease.

I eat a lot more Italian than I used to – those ladies have really started taking care of their personal hygiene.

The other night a waiter asked me for a tip. I suggested the staff shave their pubes in future – the soup had more stray hairs than a Russian gymnast.

Then the waiter asks if I want my steak 'well done'. 'Of course not, pal,' I said, 'do a cack-handed job of it, there's no point in tiring yourself out on my account.' Stupid arse.

A meal out without pudding is like a slap without a tickle.

God knows how the Chinese have got as far as they have. It takes a pretty stupid nation to declare rice a national dish and then try and eat it with sticks. Bunch of masochists.

I'm not big on pasta in restaurants. Only an Italian could charge you a couple of quid to open a tin of Heinz, robbing bastards.

I ended up dining out a lot when I was married. Anything so I didn't have to go home and see the wife's miserable face.

There's a new Korean place opened up near the station, but I don't really fancy it. It wouldn't be the first time I'd got my lips around a dog, mind you...

There used to be one of those roadside vans up our way, you could pick up all sorts from it. Salmonella, botulism, scurvy...

SCIENCE

Just because Gene is a man of action doesn't mean he hasn't got time for some of the more scientific things in life.

Like studying racing form?

There's nothing wrong with scientists; of course there ain't much right with 'em either.

I invented something once: the bruise-free groin slap.

Scientists spend their whole lives trying to discover the meaning of life. I could save them the time and bother, as it's all very simple: the less you think about it, the easier it is.

Forensic science is coming on in leaps and bounds. Give it another ten years and it might even be able to tell me something I didn't already know.

I never understood science at school. Beyond the blowing-things-up stage it just didn't appeal.

Scientists think too much, it's never healthy.

SMOKING

The Guv is a man who enjoys bad habits.

That the film about them

His favourite is probably smoking. *lezza nuns?*

People say cigarettes stink. They want to try living in Manchester, they use them as air fresheners there.

Apparently smoking makes you impotent. If that's true I hate to think what I'd be like if I quit, none of my trousers would fit.

Apparently a lot of people smoke after sex. Maybe I'm just not doing it fast enough.

Some idiots like to tell me smoking is bad for me, which is funny since pointing that out all the time is about the worst thing they could do for their own health.

I smoke a lot, but then when you find a real skill it seems a shame not to fulfil your potential.

If they made cigarettes bigger and heavier, think how much healthier we'd be. Smokable barbells, that's the way forward...

How can cigarettes be bad for you? Leaves, innit? Smoking's just like eating lots of greens.

I was once asked how many cigarettes I smoke a day. It's tricky to say, to be honest. I tend to think more in terms of how many lighters I get through, it's easier than remembering all those big numbers.

You can tell a part-time smoker: he's the sort that lights a cigarette after a meal rather than during.

TALKING TO FELLOW OFFICERS

Being a senior officer isn't just about making the big decisions, it's also about running a team of other officers, giving them advice, inspiring them to improve and making them feel valued by their fellow policemen.

That's right, you bucket of whippet shit, which is why you'll never get to my rank. You just haven't got the skills.

When I need advice from a lobotomized Essex girl I'll ask for it, OK?

I'm pumping you back up to D.S. This time make it stand for 'detective sergeant', not 'dog shit'.

If I worried as much as you, I'd never fart for fear of shitting myself.

You so much as belch out of line and I'll have your scrotum on a barbed-wire plate.

You great soft, sissy, girly, nancy, French, bender, Man United-supporting poof!

Me organ-grinder, you monkey.

They reckon you've got concussion, but I don't give a tart's furry cup if half your brains are falling out, don't ever walk into my kingdom acting like you're king of the jungle.

TECHNOLOGY

You have to move with the times and stay at the cutting edge of technology in this job.

The only cutting edge you've been near lately is a safety razor - bet your mam kept an eye on you even then.

They say the future's in computers. Not true, I kicked mine off the desk this morning and there was nothing in there but wire and fag ash.

They're putting phones in cars these days. Like the girls need something else to distract them while they're driving.

Whoever created the Walkman was a genius; now you can spot an absolute twat in seconds just by clocking the headphones.

The problem with technology is the people who use it. Shiny gadgets are to dickheads what a sheep's arse is to a Welshman.

Once you have a new piece of technology you can't imagine having lived without it.
Take photocopiers – how we managed to photograph our own arseholes in the old days I'll never know.

Whoever came up with the name 'walkie-talkie' was having a laugh, though I suppose 'shouty-crappy' doesn't have quite the same ring to it.

I've no problem with getting technology to work. You use it the same way you use teenagers, whack it hard enough and it starts working.

there
should be
more of
this on
telly

We're such good detectives, we should get our own TV show - we'd kick ass with my ninja skills.

TELEVISION

Even a hardworking copper gets a few hours off every now and then. What better way of relaxing than putting your feet up in front of the goggle box?

Charlie's Angels' Cheryl Ladd — I'd crawl half a mile over broken glass just to throw pebbles at her shit.

They don't put much on television for a man of my tastes, legal reasons, I guess.

Some people believe everything they see on television. I hate to burst their bubble but unless the next episode of **Juliet Bravo** contains nothing but an hour of Inspector Darbly scrubbing puke from the cell floors, it's still just fiction.

I could move into television if I ever retired – imagine **It's a Knockout** but with automatic weapons. Genius, that's me.

In this job I don't get much time to watch television – I suppose there had to be some perks.

Now I'm in London, people are always asking me if **Coronation Street** is what Manchester's really like. 'Of course,' I tell them, 'bar the knife fights, crack whores and story, it's spot on.'

I went on television once, can't say it was a great success. I'm sure a few housewives swooned to see me in their living rooms, but then I'm used to that.

People tell kids that watching television sends you blind, but then they tell me that about my favourite hobby and I prove 'em wrong time and time again.

I've been in the TV business for years – people will insist on nicking the things.

That **Doctor Who**'s Tardis is amazing, bigger on the inside – I knew a woman like that once.

Softly Softly? Not a good name for a police show. The only thing soft about policing is a PC's brain.

I was on telly last night, singing 'The Wild Rover'. I fell off during the first chorus, broke a standard lamp and a coffee table. Really must cut down on my drinking.

I watch a bit of football on the telly, which is not the same as being there but at least it beats the radio. Listening to football is about as satisfying as sniffing sex.

Mary Whitehouse is always banging on about how television's too violent and filled with lewd sex. I'm buggered if I can find any of it, how come she gets all the good stuff?

It's a crime that a man of my looks and talent is only likely to be seen on the bloody news.

I came across that Farrah Fawcett on telly last night. I really shouldn't have been standing so close to the screen.

More photos of Drake for here!

I found these in your drawer, Ray,
will they do?

WOMEN

DCI Gene Hunt has always had a soft spot for the ladies. *Not that soft!*

Being a smooth-talking sort he often manages to impress! *Anyone would think you fancy him yourself!*

Blimey, if that skirt was hitched up any higher I could see what you had for breakfast.

You give a bloke a gun and it's a dream come true. You give a girl one and she moans that it doesn't go with her dress.

So he pushed a bird out of a car. That doesn't make him a bad bloke.

I love women. A couple of times a day, if they'll let me.

She wants me, poor bitch.

How many women does it take to change a light bulb? Two – one to run around screaming 'What do I do? What do I do?' and one to shag the electrician.

Don't be put off by my aftershave. Underneath I'm a very nice man.

Girls love making up names for their fella, don't they? I'll admit I did have a pet name for the wife... Fido.

I'm the sort of man who is very concerned with a woman's feelings, or, to be clearer, I am very concerned with feeling women.

Get a waft of that - man stink! See if that doesn't moisten your gusset.

I have no problem with talking to women, it's very important when you're trying to agree a price.

Women are a bit like fast food. If you can get it in your mouth within five minutes it's likely to taste bad and be hazardous to your health.

I know some men aren't understanding about women's issues. Regular as clockwork something horrible spews out of their orifice and they have to take measures. When I was married I used to try and be supportive, but she didn't appreciate it. Apparently tampons aren't meant for the gob.

I love listening to women, when we're having sex anyway. I'll admit it can get a bit monotonous after that.

A lot of men say it's important to get inside a woman's head. I must admit I tend to aim lower.

I don't mind seeing things from a woman's point of view. Sometimes it's great when they go on top.

I always wore the trousers in my marriage. I tried to take them off once or twice but she was never interested.

What have I got against women? In an ideal world, nothing but my jiggling balls...

DC ~~CHRIS~~ SKELTON – As well as ~~being~~
a highly trained, ~~kung fu death-machine,~~
Skelton is a real ~~hit with~~ the ladies, who love
his ~~rugged~~ good looks and ~~brilliant~~ penis.

DC Chris Skelton likes nothing more
than a hard night in the public lavs,
taking it like a man.
He wishes his mummy had made him a
girl so he could wear nice dresses.

DS RAY CARLING - London's hardest
copper. Girls love his moustache and
curls, and have been known to orgasm
just by sniffing his musk.